HIP-HOP

50 Cent

Ashanti

Beyoncé

Mary J. Blige

Chris Brown

Mariah Carey

Sean "Diddy"
Combs

Dr. Dre

Missy Elliott

Eminem

Hip-Hop:
A Short History

Jay-Z

Alicia Keys

LL Cool J

Ludacris

Nelly

Notorious B.I.G.

Queen Latifah

Reverend Run
(Run-D.M.C.)

Will Smith

Snoop Dogg

Tupac

Usher

Kanye West

Pharrell Williams

LL Cool J

Brian Baughan

Mason Crest Publishers

Kanye West

FRONTIS Kanye West is a good example of how hip-hop reaches beyond music. The megastar is shown here attending a 2004 benefit for arts education.

PRODUCED BY 21ST CENTURY PUBLISHING AND COMMUNICATIONS, INC.

EDITORIAL BY HARDING HOUSE PUBLISHING SERVICES, INC.

MASON CREST PUBLISHERS INC.
370 Reed Road
Broomall, Pennsylvania 19008
(866)MCP-BOOK (toll free)
www.masoncrest.com

Printed in the U.S.A.

First Printing

9 8 7 6 5 4 3 2 1

Library of Congress Cataloging-in-Publication Data

Simons, Rae.
    Kanye West / by Rae Simons.
      p. cm. — (Hip-hop)
    Includes bibliographical references (p.   ) and index.
  Hardback edition: ISBN-13: 978-1-4222-0132-9
  Hardback edition: ISBN-10: 1-4222-0132-5
  Paperback edition: ISBN-13: 978-1-4222-0281-4
    1. West, Kanye—Juvenile literature. 2. Rap musicians—United States—
  Biography—Juvenile literature. I. Title. II. Series.
  ML3930.W42S56 2007
  782.421649092—dc22   2006006588

Contents

Hip-Hop Timeline   6

1 "Greatest of All Time"   9

2 Representing Queens   15

3 "Just Knock Them Out"   25

4 Mr. Smith   31

5 Looking Back, Stepping Forward   37

6 "A Pioneer and a Legend"   49

Chronology   56

Accomplishments & Awards   58

Further Reading & Internet Resources   60

Glossary   61

Index   62

Picture Credits   64

About the Author   64

Hip-Hop Timeline

1974 Hip-hop pioneer Afrika Bambaataa organizes the Universal Zulu Nation.

1988 *Yo! MTV Raps* premieres on MTV.

1970s Hip-hop as a cultural movement begins in the Bronx, New York City.

1985 *Krush Groove*, a hip-hop film about Def Jam Recordings, is released featuring Run-D.M.C., Kurtis Blow, LL Cool J, and the Beastie Boys.

1970s DJ Kool Herc pioneers the use of breaks, isolations, and repeats using two turntables.

1979 The Sugarhill Gang's song "Rapper's Delight" is the first hip-hop single to go gold.

1986 Run-D.M.C. are the first rappers to appear on the cover of *Rolling Stone* magazine.

1970   1980   1988

1976 Grandmaster Flash & the Furious Five pioneer hip-hop MCing and freestyle battles.

1986 Beastie Boys' album *Licensed to Ill* is released and becomes the best-selling rap album of the 1980s.

1970s Break dancing emerges at parties and in public places in New York City.

1982 Afrika Bambaataa embarks on the first European hip-hop tour.

1988 Hip-hop music annual record sales reaches $100 million.

1970s Graffiti artist Vic pioneers tagging on subway trains in New York City.

1984 *Graffiti Rock*, the first hip-hop television program, premieres.

1993 Rapper Snoop Dogg's album *Doggystyle* is the first debut album to hit the music charts at number one.

2006 Queen Latifah becomes the first hip-hop artist to receive a star on the Hollywood Walk of Fame.

1989 DJ Jazzy Jeff & The Fresh Prince become the first hip-hop artists to win a Grammy Award.

2003 Rapper Eminem becomes the first hip-hop artist to win an Academy Award.

2005 Hip-hop artist Kanye West appears on the cover of *Time* magazine.

1989 Rap is added as a new category to the *Billboard* charts.

1997 East Coast rapper Notorious B.I.G. (aka Biggie Smalls) is murdered.

2004 First National Hip-Hop Political Convention is held in Newark, New Jersey.

1989　　　　　2000　　　　　2006

1996 West Coast rapper Tupac Shakur is shot and killed.

2005 Rapper Will Smith opens the Philadelphia Live 8 concert as part of 10 simultaneous concerts held worldwide to bring attention to the extreme poverty in Africa.

1990s Hip-hop emerges in Europe.

1989 First gangsta rap album, *Straight Outta Compton*, is released by N.W.A.

2001 The hip-hop political action group, Hip-Hop Summit Action Network, is founded by Russell Simmons.

1992 Dr. Dre's album *The Chronic* is released; it redefines West Coast rap.

2006 The Smithsonian Institute National Museum of American History announces the creation of a new hip-hop exhibition scheduled to open in three to five years.

Wearing his signature Kangol hat and gold chain, LL Cool J performs during VH1's *Hip-Hop Honors* program in 2005. During the show, other rappers paid tribute to LL Cool J's long career and his contributions to hip-hop music.

1

"Greatest of All Time"

Dressed in his old-school getup—a white Kangol hat, gold chain, and a tracksuit jacket that he quickly discarded—LL Cool J commanded the stage at New York City's Hammerstein Ballroom. He spit out rhymes that mowed down the competition. "I'm gonna take this itty bitty world by storm, and I'm just gettin' warm!" he shouted.

LL Cool J had released his hit single "Mama Said Knock You Out" 14 years earlier, but his performance on the night of September 26, 2005, during the VH1 network's *Second Annual Hip-Hop Honors* program made the song as fresh as ever. As he stood on the edge of the stage, his chiseled frame looming over fans, world domination almost seemed in his grasp.

An estimated 1.4 million viewers tuned in to watch the *Second Annual Hip-Hop Honors* show celebrate the music of LL Cool J and other rap superstars like Big Daddy Kane, Ice-T, the late Notorious B.I.G., and one of the original hip-hop groups, Grandmaster Flash & the Furious Five. For the program, some of the hottest contemporary hip-hop acts paid tribute to the artists who had helped create what has become one of the world's most popular music **genres**.

Multi-platinum rapper Nelly was picked to give the tribute to LL Cool J, which included a version of "I'm Bad," a classic released back in 1987. Nelly played the part well, also sporting an old-school outfit with thick gold chain, a white tracksuit, and a Kangol hat (LL never takes off his hat onstage). Joining him on the turntable was Cut Creator, LL's own DJ for the past two decades. How did Nelly pull off his spot-on imitation? Because for years LL has been the performer Nelly and his peers have tried to imitate. "Man, I've been doing LL my whole life," the rapper explained to a reporter.

When it was LL's turn to take the stage that night, he was in special company. Not only were his loyal fans in the audience, there was also Sean "P. Diddy" Combs; LL's movie costar and fellow rapper, Queen Latifah; and some of the rappers who inspired him so long ago. In fact, when Grandmaster Flash & the Furious Five stormed the stage to perform "Freedom" and "The Message," LL became just another fan again. Occasional shots of him in the audience showed him rapping word for word to "The Message," just as he had when he was a kid growing up in Hollis, a neighborhood of the New York City borough of Queens.

Having a place among hip-hop pioneers is quite a privilege, but LL stands above even this select group, because unlike Grandmaster Flash & the Furious Five, Big Daddy Kane, and Ice-T, this MC is *still* in the game. LL Cool J has 12 albums under his belt—seven of which were multi-platinum records (selling more than 2 million copies). For the other rappers, the VH1 *Hip-Hop Honors* was a chance to relive past glories. For LL, it was just another show, another KO.

I Need a Label

More than two decades earlier, James Todd Smith, a.k.a. LL Cool J, recorded his first demo, a track called "I Need a Beat." Back then he was a shy, skinny 16-year-old who did not cut an imposing figure. But he was determined to get a label deal, and he had the rhyming skills to do it. It was not long before he teamed up with Rick Rubin and Russell Simmons, the original owners of the rap label Def Jam, and secured his place in hip-hop history. When the cuts from his bare-boned 1985

Rapper Nelly is called on stage to perform his version of an LL Cool J song at the 2005 *VH1 Hip-Hop Honors*. Like many current rappers, Nelly had grown up listening to LL Cool J's music.

debut *Radio* hit the airwaves, they launched the label that for the next two decades would release albums by acts like the Beastie Boys, Public Enemy, DMX, Jay-Z, and Kanye West.

Between the releases of *Radio* and his latest album, *Todd Smith*, in March 2006, this winner of two Grammys has maintained his status as one of hip-hop's biggest stars, with stellar albums like *Bigger and Deffer* (1987), *Mama Said Knock You Out* (1990), *Mr. Smith* (1995),

LL Cool J (center) signs a new record deal with Def Jam Music in 2003; Def Jam founder Russell Simmons is seated on the left. LL was Def Jam's first big star, and his popularity made the label among the most important in hip-hop.

and *10* (2002). In a field of entertainment where performers rarely stick around too long, LL has shown remarkable endurance. He is also a **versatile** artist: ever since recording the ballad "I Need Love" on *Bigger and Deffer*, his audience has known him as a smooth operator as well as a formidable MC. (His sculpted figure, which he rarely hesitates to display onstage, has never hurt his image with his female fans, either.)

From early on it seemed that superstardom was in LL's grasp, but to reach it the rapper has also had to overcome many obstacles in his life. He has been frank with the public about these challenges, which include overcoming a history of abuse as a child. While succeeding as a rapper has not posed serious challenges for LL Cool J, other aspects of life have. Today, LL fans know him as someone who can conquer the world but also keep it real by wrestling with the demons of the past.

Having survived many trials inside and outside the entertainment world, Todd Smith is now a mature veteran with much wisdom to offer his audience and the next generation of rappers. From Hollis to Hollywood and back, this veteran has traveled far to claim his hip-hop honors.

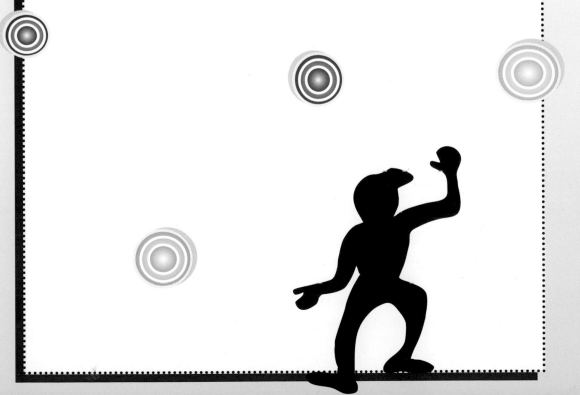

Todd Smith grew up in a tough Queens neighborhood. Though his childhood was not easy, he was fortunate to have a loving mother and caring grandparents, who did their best to watch out for him while he was growing up.

2

Representing Queens

Although known for ripping rivals to shreds with his lyrics, LL Cool J has also handed out his share of compliments, even for his grandmother. Some may call an MC soft for rapping about his grandma, but Ellen Griffin was an extraordinary woman. She was not only LL's artistic inspiration, she was a great source of support and one of his best friends.

It was Ellen and her husband, Eugene, who opened up their home in Queens to Todd and his mother, Ondrea, when they needed a place to live after Ondrea separated from Todd's abusive father, James. Todd, then four years old, was fine with moving from his home in Brentwood, Long Island, where his family had moved after his birth in January 1968. He had always loved spending time at his grandparents' house, and now it was home. Before long it was clear that Eugene and Ellen would be loyal family during the best and worst times, including the night James came looking for his estranged wife.

Violent Days

James had shown up at Todd's grandparents' late one evening demanding that Ondrea take him back. She had no interest in discussing the issue, and her dismissal made him angry. He pulled out a 12-gauge shotgun and started shooting into the doorway. Todd ran in from where he was sleeping in the back room to find blood everywhere. Ondrea had been hit in the lower back. Eugene, who had tried to intervene, took a shot in the stomach.

In a miraculous feat of strength, Ellen Griffin hoisted both her husband and daughter into the backseat of her car and drove them to the hospital. Their lives were saved, but they both spent time in recovery. Eugene, who suffered intestinal damage, underwent surgery and came home after a few weeks. However, Todd's mother was in worse shape. With her lower back traumatized by the shotgun pellets, she was temporarily paralyzed and remained in the hospital for six months.

An arrest warrant was filed against James, who ran to California, but the charges were later dropped. Somehow, Ondrea was able to forgive him. He was never prosecuted for the attempted murders.

Even with his father out of the picture, Todd's childhood was still plagued by violence. Shortly after Ondrea recovered from her injuries, she married another abusive man named Roscoe. Although Roscoe was a more **civil** husband to Ondrea, he was a horrible stepfather to Todd. In his autobiography *I Make My Own Rules*, LL describes Roscoe abusing him on a regular basis, either hitting him with his bare fists or using weapons like extension cords and vacuum cleaner attachments. During one episode Roscoe threw Todd outside without a coat on a cold winter day because he had asked for something to eat. By the time he was nine, Todd was desperate for a way to get his mind off the cruelty he was suffering.

Two Turntables and a Microphone

Music offered the release Todd was looking for. What particularly grabbed him was a new sound at the time called rap. Recognizing their grandson's new passion, Ellen and Eugene bought him two turntables, a set of speakers, a mixer, and a microphone. Soon Todd began making beats of his own to rhyme over.

In those days any rapper looking to make a name for himself needed a DJ, and Todd found the most popular one in Queens, Jay Philpot. The two became friends and were soon performing at

LL COOL J

with Karen Hunter

I MAKE MY OWN RULES

The autobiography *I Make My Own Rules* was LL Cool J's chance to tell his story and explore his life. In the book he described many experiences that he had never previously discussed publicly, such as being beaten as a child.

neighborhood block parties. They also started making tapes, and under the name Ladies Love Cool James, Todd sent dozens of demo tapes to major labels. At first Cool James faced nothing but rejection slips—enough to "start a fire," he remembers. But one day Rick Rubin, a New York University student and **novice** producer looking for some talent, responded to LL's submission and arranged to get together with him.

Shortly after getting past the shock that Rubin was a white Jewish man ("Yo! I thought you were black!" were the first words out of LL's mouth when he met him), LL and his new partner got to work. Rubin played a few beats he had recorded with his drum machine, and LL liked what he heard. He immediately began writing lyrics. Rubin then offered some feedback, and in no time they cut a demo that they were both excited about.

The only remaining concern was the rapper's name. In Rubin's mind, "Ladies Love Cool James" was too long, and he asked if could be shortened. "I was like, whatever," LL said in an interview years later with CNN. "It could have been whatever he wanted it to be, you know, Jethro. I'd have still made the album."

Rubin tried to persuade his friend Russell Simmons, then a manager for Run-D.M.C. and other up-and-coming acts, that they should do a studio recording and release the album themselves. Simmons hesitated at first, because he was hoping to forge a partnership with a larger company rather than start an independent label. But Rubin insisted that the two could do better on their own, and Simmons became convinced. "I Need a Beat" was released in November 1984 as Def Jam's first official release and the first single off LL's debut, *Radio*.

Several other singles followed, including "I Can't Live Without My Radio" and "Rock the Bells." LL's lyrics on "I Can't Live Without My Radio" and other tracks never strayed far from his experiences in Queens or his passion for rap music:

> **"My story is rough, my neighborhood is tough**
> **But I still sport gold, and I'm out to crush**
> **My name is Cool J, I devastate the show**
> **But I couldn't survive without my radio."**

It wasn't long before *Radio* hit the airwaves. In his book, LL describes what it was like to be a 16-year-old kid hearing himself on the radio for

Russell Simmons and Rick Rubin founded the Def Jam music label in the early 1980s, signing LL Cool J as their first act. Simmons and Rubin are in the center of this 2001 photo with rappers Noreaga (now called NORE) and Capone.

the first time. "It was like time had slowed down," he remembers, "the Earth was spinning half time and it was just me and my record."

In April 1986 Ellen Griffin was the first to receive the call that *Radio* had gone gold (selling more than 500,000 copies). From the beginning she closely followed her grandson's career (she even offered useful feedback on some of his recordings). She was proud of LL, but at the same time she was concerned. His late night shows were keeping him from getting up in the morning for school, and he was making other excuses not to attend classes at all. She decided to put her foot down and told him he had to move out if was not going to get an education. LL chose to pursue music and took an offer from his manager to crash at his place. Dropping out of a school was a decision that LL would regret once he realized he lacked basic money-managing skills. And by the time that happened, serious amounts of cash were starting to roll in.

Ballads and BMWs

By 1987 LL and the public were ready for another album, which arrived in June of that year. *Bigger and Deffer* went double platinum in only a few months, and with its hit "I Need Love," LL now could claim the distinction of recording the first rap ballad. Although Rick Rubin

LL Cool J poses with Bobcat, E. Love, and Cut Creator backstage at the 1988 Soul Train Music Awards program. That night LL Cool J won for the crossover single "I Need Love" and the double platinum album *Bigger and Deffer*.

and Russell Simmons were not so eager at first to see Def Jam's star rapper readily show his sensitive side, LL wisely stuck to his guns. "I Need Love" became the first rap song to top *Billboard*'s R&B singles chart. This made him a crossover hit and brought his music to an even wider audience.

Love was on LL's mind a lot during that time. On Easter Sunday 1987 he met Simone Johnson, his first steady girlfriend. He immediately bonded with her because she was from his neighborhood and faced circumstances like his own growing up. But the life of a rap star who is always on the road came with plenty of temptations, and during those initial years, LL had trouble staying committed to Simone.

The lures of the music business also enticed him to carelessly spend his new money. "I've been ridiculous with it," he said in a December

From the moment they met in 1987, LL Cool J and Simone Johnson were meant to be together. They were not married until 1995, however. By that time, Simone and LL had two children and a third on the way.

The release of *Bigger and Deffer* made LL Cool J a rich man. He was making more money than either he or his staff knew how to handle. The addition of his estranged father to the management team did not help the situation.

2002 interview with the hip-hop magazine *The Source*. Listing sports cars among his major vices, he remembered a few times walking into a car dealership and buying a Porsche or a BMW on the spot.

During that time, a crew of advisers, managers, and accountants were giving LL poor financial advice. Their planning often neglected the taxes that he eventually would have to pay on his sizable income. LL's mother, who was acting as his manager, was overwhelmed with the accounting tasks she was facing and eventually made the bold decision to call her ex-husband for assistance. Despite James's regrettable history with the family, Ondrea felt his experience as a former business owner would be an asset. LL, of course, was wary about letting his dad be a part of life again, and James, it turned out, would handle his responsibilities poorly.

LL Cool J was unaware of his financial problems, though. He felt that his music career was still on course and was sure that he had enough money. On top of the two albums that had already gone platinum, he had also charted with the single "Going Back to Cali," which appeared on the soundtrack for the thriller *Less Than Zero*.

Walking With a Panther, his third album, came out in 1989. However, its sales didn't meet his label's high expectations, even though the first single, "I'm That Type of Guy," went gold. Some critics said that the album, with three ballads, was missing that "street" sound of his first two efforts. On tour, audiences agreed, and he sometimes faced boos.

Out on the road, LL was tempted, among other things, by drugs. He now looks back on this period as his most destructive, and in his autobiography, he remembers one night when he performed high on **mescaline**. In recounting that period when he was using, he says he found "no answers, just a question: Why?"

Although taking drugs left him ill-prepared for fatherhood, LL's first child, Najee, was born to Simone in 1989. Would he settle down with Simone and help raise their baby? As the 1990s approached, it was not clear where LL was headed.

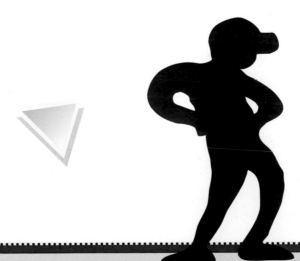

By 1990 LL Cool J's career seemed in need of a boost—*Rolling Stone* noted that there were "insults to be avenged." The rapper's album *Mama Said Knock You Out*, inspired by advice from his grandmother, proved that LL was still a rapper with attitude.

3

"Just Knock Them Out"

Toward the end of the 1980s, a new form of hip-hop called gangsta rap was sparking controversy and selling millions of records. With their unapologetic boasts about living the gangster life, west coast rappers like Ice-T and N.W.A were rapidly gaining ground in the hip-hop world. LL Cool J and other rappers like Run-D.M.C. suddenly seemed less hard.

LL realized that if he released another mediocre album like *Walking With a Panther*, it could ruin his career. While mulling over his next move, he turned to his grandmother, Ellen. In her mind worrying about the competition was not an option. Her response—"Oh, baby, just knock them out!"—planted the seed for one of hip-hop's most well-known tracks. The album *Mama Said Knock You Out* was released in August 1990. As an album that was, in LL's own words, "not gangsta, just hard," it answered the challenge of his rivals.

With the help of a new producer, Marley Marl, LL crafted what *Rolling Stone* called a "hip-hop masterpiece." Although the album was a return to his raw delivery, he still made sure not to neglect his romantic side. He even managed to land a spot on the show MTV *Unplugged*, a concert series that typically featured quieter acoustic acts. LL was a shoe-in for the Grammy for Best Rap Solo Performance, which he took home for "Mama Said Knock You Out" in February 1991.

But there was no time to bask in the media spotlight. "I'm working on a platinum career, not a platinum album," LL said in an interview with *Rolling Stone*. Ready to expand his success into other areas of entertainment, he dove headfirst into movie acting. His first notable role was as a cop in *The Hard Way*, an action comedy starring Michael J. Fox and James Woods. The following year he acted alongside Robin Williams in the comedy *Toys*. These were only supporting roles, but they offered the start LL was looking for.

A New Drug

While the public LL Cool J was faring well, the private one still had personal commitments to fulfill. With the birth of his daughter, Italia, in 1990, there were now two children he was not spending time with. Making the situation worse, he had become involved with another woman. Fortunately, when it seemed LL most needed help, a spiritually minded associate of Russell Simmons named Charles Fisher walked into LL's life and offered him an alternative to his champagne-and-women lifestyle.

In his book LL writes that during that period he thought he was living the good life. "But underneath the gold chains and the glitter was this foul stench," he wrote. "And I guess Charles smelled it." LL compared himself to "a junkie needing a fix, and [Charles] had the drug—knowledge."

After some hesitation LL began reading the Bible, the Qur'an, and other spiritual literature that Charles recommended to him. His mentor also asked him to take part in community work and convinced him to be honorary chairman for Youth Enterprises, a program for disadvantaged youth. It was a great experience that inspired LL to start his own organization for kids, Camp Cool J, in August 1992. Through the program, 15 to 30 inner-city youths with exceptional grades were able to attend a year-round camp where they participated in educational, cultural, and recreational programs. LL also took part in the

There was a lot to celebrate in 1991. LL Cool J won the MTV Video Music Award for Best Rap Video for "Mama Said Knock You Out." He later won a Grammy Award for Best Rap Solo Performance for the same song.

launch of AmeriCorps, a national volunteer organization initiated by President Bill Clinton in 1993.

14 Shots

Good things were emerging from LL's soul-searching during this time, but it was also difficult work. In his autobiography, he remembers breaking down in tears at one point. "I was crying for a woman I had

Thanks to his mentor Charles Fisher, LL Cool J began exploring his spirituality. Fisher helped the rapper recognize his personal problems. His darkest album, *14 Shots to the Dome*, became part of his soul-searching effort.

treated like a dog, crying for the children I had abandoned, crying for my life, which I was just throwing away," he wrote. Clearly, the days of running from his responsibilities were catching up with him.

This time of **introspection** produced another album, *14 Shots to the Dome*, which was by far LL Cool J's darkest recording and, in his view, the deepest thing he had ever done lyrically. Although it still had the party jams expected from any LL record, it also featured "Crossroads," a moody track that painted a picture of his troubled mind at the time.

But listeners did not seem ready for such brutal honesty from LL. The album sold 800,000 copies—an impressive number for some artists, but not for one who already had gone platinum four times. Meanwhile, his movie career was not faring any better. Although he got the starring role he was looking for in the thriller *Out-of-Sync*, the movie bombed at the box office. According to LL, it should have gone straight to video.

With his income as an entertainer taking a momentary slide, LL needed good financial expertise. He knew, however, that was something he could not get from his father or the rest of his management team, whose criminally poor planning meant he owed $2 million in back taxes. LL realized that the only person he trusted to manage his money was himself, but without a high school education, he knew he lacked the skills to take care of his finances. At age 27, he was finally ready to go back to school.

LL Cool J and his wife Simone bring their children Italia and Samaria to the premiere of *S.W.A.T.* It had become clear to LL that what was missing in his life was commitment to his family, so in 1995 he asked Simone to marry him.

4

Mr. Smith

The year 1995 marked a turnaround for LL. He was ready to be Todd Smith again, a regular guy making the tough decisions that LL Cool J had put off. He fired his father; he enrolled in a **G.E.D.** program to get his high school diploma; and he married his girlfriend—the mother of his two children.

"I realized that the love I was seeking was there all along. It had been there for more than eight years," LL wrote of his decision to propose to Simone. They were married in August 1995. It was a small, quiet ceremony at their home in Merrick, Long Island. Soon after the wedding, LL and Simone had their third child, daughter Samaria. With the older kids getting involved in sports, LL Cool J was now ready to be a soccer dad.

Enrolling in a G.E.D. program, a decision that undoubtedly made his grandmother proud, cleared up more unfinished business. It was a humbling move for someone with a Grammy and four platinum albums, but he knew he had to receive training to better manage his finances and boost his confidence in handling business affairs. While taking the classes, he also continued discussing his new spirituality with his mentor Charles Fisher.

Another Break

With many of his personal matters settled, LL next moved on to improving his acting career. The right opportunity presented itself when Quincy Jones, a renowned musician, composer, and television producer, offered him a starring role in a television sitcom. LL was excited by the opportunity because he knew Jones had already helped rapper Will Smith become established with his own sitcom, *The Fresh Prince of Bel-Air*, and he was eager to follow in Smith's footsteps. "Today I see Will Smith in blockbuster films, having become a box office superstar," he wrote in his autobiography, "and I respect how he **parlayed** his rap career into a big-time film career."

LL's show, *In the House*, first aired on NBC in April 1995. It was about a man named Marion Hill, a cash-strapped former football star and landlord who befriends his **tenants**. Along with relating to the character's financial woes, LL was impressed with Marion's positive stance. "What really convinced me to do the show was the character had a **holistic** approach to life—no drinking, no wild women, no drugs," he wrote. The show lasted for only one season on NBC, but the UPN network then offered to pick it up, where it had better success and lasted for three more years. The last episode aired in 1999.

On the music front, the release of *Mr. Smith* in November 1995—the same month LL and Def Jam celebrated their 10th anniversary together—marked another comeback. The pressure had been on once again, and if it were not for some timely advice from his peers, LL might have released a dud. Lyor Cohen, then president of Def Jam, made some suggestions to LL and brought in producer Chris Lighty, who set the rapper up with another pair of producers who went by the promising name Trackmasters. LL liked his new collaborations with the producers, particularly "I Shot Ya," a track that was a change of pace for him because it featured several rappers, including Fat Joe and Foxy Brown. It was not long before he scrapped most of the original album in favor of the new material.

Two singles off *Mr. Smith*, "Loungin" and the 1996 summer hit "Doin It," found play on the radio, but even more popular was the romantic rap "Hey Lover," a duet with the R&B group Boyz II Men. A *Rolling Stone* review singled out "Hey Lover," saying that "what on paper seems like schmaltz ends up being one of the most worthwhile tracks LL has ever committed to tape." "Hey Lover" became LL Cool J's first single to go platinum, and it earned him his second Grammy for Best Rap Solo Performance.

At the premiere of *Deliver Us from Eva*, LL Cool J poses with fellow rapper Will Smith. Smith had gone from a career in rap music to starring roles in television shows and movies, and LL hoped to emulate him.

LL Cool J has had one of the longest-lived careers in the hip-hop world. However, the rapper's detractors have always been ready to claim that LL was washed up—a charge he attempted to answer with his album *Mr. Smith* (1995).

Because *Mr. Smith* accentuated LL's softer side, he was finding more popularity with the R&B audience. To expand that appeal, he teamed up with R&B acts R. Kelly and the group Solo for the Down Low Tour. Life on the road no longer put temptations in LL's way. This time out he was on a mission, and he devoted as much time as he could to community work and visiting hospitals, schools, and churches in every city. During one particular hospital visit, he met an abused boy who had been badly burned in a house fire. As harrowing as the experience was, it only stirred LL to do more. "I realized not only that this boy was someone I wanted to look out for, but that there are millions of kids out there, and they're all special," he wrote.

Set in a new direction as a married man, happy father, television star, and **humanitarian**, LL Cool J had reached a place few people could have anticipated a few years earlier. When he heard the news that *Mr. Smith* had gone platinum in January 1996, it seemed that everything was moving forward. Receiving his second Grammy award the following month was even more rewarding. "The feeling of winning that Grammy—it was like regaining the heavyweight championship of the world," he wrote.

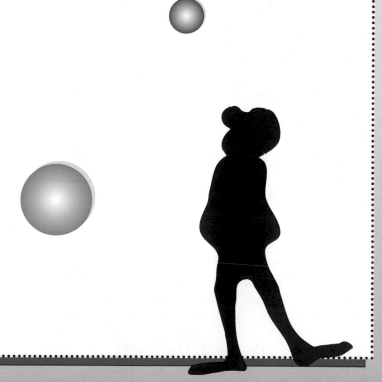

During the mid-1990s, LL Cool J took some time to look back over his life and career, while stepping forward musically. In 1997 he released two auto-biographical projects, the album *Phenomenon* and the book *I Make My Own Rules*.

‹5›

Looking Back, Stepping Forward

By September 1996, *Mr. Smith* had become LL Cool J's third multi-platinum album. Few artists could boast that level of success—in hip-hop or any genre. Considering that he had extended a rap career of that caliber for over a decade, it only seemed right to look back on what brought him to this point.

In November 1996 he released a greatest-hits album that brought together all his best tracks. And in 1997 he continued to look back, simultaneously releasing an autobiographical album, *Phenomenon*, and an autobiographical book, *I Make My Own Rules*.

A good portion of LL's seventh studio album, *Phenomenon*, explored the joys and pains of his personal past. In the lighthearted "Candy," he relived his years of teenage romance, and in "Father," the album's biggest hit, he narrates the shooting of his mother and grandfather and the beatings he suffered from his stepfather. These lines from the third verse of "Father" describe the shooting:

Co-authored by Karen Hunter, the autobiography was made available in two versions—one that was "suitable for all audiences" and another for older readers that contained more **explicit** details about LL's sex life. In a December 1997 review of the book, *Vibe* magazine said, "LL's unflinching autobiography dives deeply into life experiences." They gave the rapper an A-plus "for his heartfelt, revealing effort." Readers were impressed, too. It became a national bestseller.

At a book signing in New York City in 1997, rapper LL Cool J gives Kenan Malkic, a 15-year-old Bosnian severely wounded by a land mine, an autographed copy of his book *I Make My Own Rules*.

I Make My Own Rules naturally racked up sales because it was a behind-the-scenes look at a megastar, but the book turned out to be much more than just another tell-all **memoir**. In its introduction LL stated the many reasons he had for writing the book. One was self-driven: in wrestling with his troubled past, he hoped to "keep it real" with himself and find some resolution. "I started writing this book for myself. As therapy, an emotional and spiritual cleansing," he explained. But there were also several groups he hoped the book would reach, including child victims of abuse, those who LL believed misunderstood rap music, and African Americans who were looking for a closer understanding of their culture so that they can know "where they come from" and "embrace America on their own terms."

For the kids, LL doled out plenty of lessons without being preachy. He owned up to using drugs early in his career and briefly dabbling in drug dealing but had stern words for those looking to follow in his footsteps. "The dealer's life has many entrances. But the only two exits are prison and death. Remember that," he wrote.

LL also wanted to address the connections that some people make between rap and gang violence. It was a controversial topic, because in the past year hip-hop had lost two great rappers, Tupac Shakur and the Notorious B.I.G., to drive-by shootings. LL recognized that there was a deep-seated problem facing the rap community, but he took politicians and other leaders to task for jumping to conclusions. He accused them of putting the blame for gang violence on rap music when there were so many other forces contributing to gang-related crime like poverty, joblessness, and the need for self-protection.

Switching Gears

With the success of *I Make My Own Rules*, LL could add "accomplished writer" to his résumé. He also had fared well on television, with his sitcom *In the House* in its fourth season. But he still had not attained his goal of becoming a successful actor in movies. His only starring film role had been in the flop *Out-of-Sync*. So in June 1998, LL announced that he was putting music on the backburner to devote more time and energy to his movie career.

His new commitment paid off, as a whole series of movie roles came his way. In 1998 he appeared in the urban thriller *Caught Up*, the romantic comedy *Woo*, and the horror flick *Halloween H20*. The

THE SOURCE

THE MAGAZINE OF HIP-HOP MUSIC, CULTURE & POLITICS

100TH ISSUE

RAKIM KOOL HERC TUPAC
PUFF DADDY WU-TANG
ICE T NOTORIOUS B.I.G.
SNOOP DOGGY DOGG N.W.A
TRIBE CALLED QUEST
ROCK STEADY CREW
BRAND NUBIAN NAS
DR. DRE PUBLIC ENEMY
BIG DADDY KANE
EPMD KRS-ONE
QUEEN LATIFAH
SLICK RICK
GETO BOYS
SALT-N-PEPA
ICE CUBE
DE LA SOUL
CYPRESS HILL
MOBB DEEP
BUSTA RHYMES
OUTKAST

THE GREATEST MC
THE GREATEST GROUP
THE GREATEST SONG
THE GREATEST ALBUM
THE GREATEST BEAT
THE GREATEST POSSE CUT
THE GREATEST GRAF ARTIST
THE GREATEST DJ
THE GREATEST FILM
THE GREATEST DANCE STEP
THE GREATEST TOUR
THE GREATEST LYRICIST
THE GREATEST PRODUCER
THE GREATEST B-BOY CREW

LL COOL J
FUTURE OF THE FUNK

JANUARY 1998 · NO. 100
US $ · UK £2.20 · CANADA $3.50

0 74470 78191 2

In 1998 *The Source*, a magazine devoted to hip-hop music and culture, featured LL Cool J on the cover of its 100th issue. Ironically, it was this same year that LL decided to refocus his career toward making movies in Hollywood.

following year he scored parts in another horror movie, *Deep Blue Sea*, and the crime thriller *In Too Deep*.

During 1999 he also landed a part in the football movie *Any Given Sunday*. Having played football as a kid with dreams of being an NFL star, LL had eagerly sought an audition for the part of a professional running back. After he got it, he underwent a strict training regimen to gain muscle. The movie, which was directed by Oliver Stone, was LL's biggest film yet.

Although none of the movies offered the starring role he hoped for, they did bring him plenty of exposure. By 2000 he was ready to turn back to his recording career.

LL Cool J had an important part as a football player in the hit movie *Any Given Sunday* (1999). The film was directed by Oliver Stone and also featured award-winning actor Al Pacino and talented comedian Jamie Foxx.

The Greatest

LL approached his eighth studio album with a mission: to return to his roots. To that end he made the decision to record the album in New York where he knew he would find inspiration. Talking to *The Source* in September 2000, he said: "I didn't want to be in Beverly Hills writing songs that deal with my community." To ensure the album's edgy feel, he invited hardcore rappers DMX, Redman, and Method Man to record with him again, as well as Snoop Dogg and Ja Rule.

Even with all his achievements, LL still went in the studio as if he had to prove himself. "He had the kind of hunger of a dude who just got his first deal," said DJ Scratch, who produced eight tracks on the album. The boldly titled *G.O.A.T. Featuring James T. Smith: The Greatest of All Time* hit the streets in September, debuting at number one on the record charts. During the first week, the album sold more than 208,000 copies, according to SoundScan numbers.

The album, however, did not sustain the initial level of sales through the following weeks and months. It had received mixed reviews. Some critics, still attached to his ladies' man persona, were not receptive to his return to the old sound. *The Source* said that the album was "middle of the road," and that its rage was "contrived."

LL did not dwell on the fact that *G.O.A.T.* was not well received by some critics, although he did maintain that being the hardest-sounding rapper was never his ambition in recording the album. "It wasn't about me trying to be a tough guy," he told *The Source*. "It was about me going back home."

By this time, it seemed that LL was becoming more and more familiar with going back home. With the birth of his daughter, Nina Simone, in 2000, he now had four kids, and he was acting more and more like the all-American dad, attending his kids' soccer, basketball, and lacrosse games. He grew accustomed to arguing referee calls from the sidelines.

This life as faithful husband and devoted father may not fit with the image of a rapper, but it did not seem to bother LL. Nor did he worry about losing an "edge" if he refused to rap about carrying guns. He was increasingly more interested in bringing a positive message to rap music. This was a central goal when he began recording his next album in 2002, *10*. *10* was the first major hip-hop album in some time not to come with an "explicit lyrics" sticker.

The title *10* referred to the number of albums LL had released, including his greatest hits LP. Five of the album's tracks were recorded

LL Cool J promotes his album *G.O.A.T. Featuring James T. Smith: The Greatest of All Time* at a Boston radio station. The album's title was borrowed from the boxing legend Muhammad Ali, who also called himself the Greatest of All Time.

by the hottest producers in hip-hop and R&B at the time, a duo called the Neptunes. One of these tracks, "Luv U Better," was a duet with R&B singer Marc Dorsey that became the first LL single since "I Need Love" to claim the number one spot on the R&B/Hip-hop charts. Another track, "Paradise," also received heavy radio play. A second version of *10* included "All I Have," a Jennifer Lopez song that featured LL Cool J. The song, which kept the number one spot on *Billboard*'s Hot 100 for 4 weeks, was to date LL's most successful single.

One of the cuts on *10*, "Big Mama (Unconditional Love)," was overlooked in favor of the other hits, but it nonetheless had deep personal meaning for LL. It was a heartfelt tribute to his grandmother, released

LL Cool J has long been committed to helping young people. Here, he joins other hip-hop artists at a 2002 rally in New York City to protest cuts in the budgets of city public schools.

before she passed away in November of 2002. In the best way he knew how, LL took the opportunity to publicly thank her for all she had done for him. He rapped about all the much-deserved whoopings she had given him as a boy and the much-needed tips she had given him as a rapper struggling to make it.

Feeling Better

With *10*, LL had set out to make a record that was, as he told *Billboard* magazine, "a positive record with no profanity, strong energy, and tight beats; a record that makes [one] feel better after hearing it." He was not alone in his quest to help make hip-hop a more positive music form. In June 2001 he was invited to attend the first Hip-Hop Summit, a meeting in New York City that Def Jam founder Russell Simmons organized to discuss pressing issues like First Amendment rights and the responsibility that rappers had to the country's youth. In addition to LL, rappers like Sean "P. Diddy" Combs and Public Enemy's Chuck D were in attendance to hear from prominent figures like Harvard professor Cornel West and Nation of Islam leader Louis Farrakhan.

LL heeded Farrakhan's **exhortation** that rappers "accept the responsibility [they've] never accepted" as leaders to their young fans. "It doesn't matter how good you're supposed to be at what you do," LL told MTV News. "If you can't inspire people to be positive and be leaders and dream, you're not utilizing the power that you have for the best."

It was ironic that as millions of records by this self-dubbed "Greatest of All Time" were still selling, LL Cool J was now more humble than ever, imagining how he could best inspire his fans and move hip-hop forward. In fact, it seemed he was just grateful that he still had the chance to rock the mic. "I'm very appreciative that people enjoy what I'm doing," he told *Ebony* magazine in 2003. "All I can do is just give them the best that I can give them."

To celebrate LL Cool J's re-signing with Def Jam, the CEO of the New York Stock Exchange invites Russell Simmons and LL to ring the opening bell. LL had been looking at other record labels, but he and Def Jam came to a mutually beneficial agreement.

◄6►

"A Pioneer and a Legend"

For those who were not already convinced, the events of 2003 confirmed that LL Cool J was here to stay as a performer. After taking home honors at the Soul Train Awards as well as the NAACP Image Awards, he received a Grammy nomination for "Luv U Better" in the Rap/Sung Collaboration category.

Afterwards, Def Jam renewed its recording contract with LL. The decision came after an anxious period of negotiating with other labels, but when LL signed on the dotted line, the partnership between the biggest label in rap and the "Greatest of All Time" was sealed once again. When the new contract was announced, Russell Simmons took the opportunity to sing praises of the man who sold over 20 million records with Def Jam and helped bring hip-hop into the mainstream. Simmons said:

"LL Cool J is a shining example of the longevity and power of hip-hop. In fact, he is the embodiment of hip-hop. He is one of the architects of the Def Jam culture. I am privileged to work with a man who is both a pioneer and a legend. **"**

Platinum Career

The "platinum career" LL had sought had become a reality, and as he had planned, it included success as an actor and writer as well as a rapper. In 2002 LL Cool J's second book, *And the Winner Is*, was published. The children's story, a tale of good sportsmanship on the basketball court, invites kids to read and rap along to the CD that accompanies the book. A separate instrumental track leaves space for readers to come up with their own rhymes that reflect on the book's content. LL's inspiration for writing the book came from watching his kids play sports. He saw that the playing field is a great place to illustrate lessons about winning and losing with grace.

The very existence of a "rap-along" book was proof of the great appeal hip-hop had gained with all groups and ages, in large part owing to the mainstream success of rappers like LL Cool J. The book also showed how eager LL was to reach young readers with positive messages and lessons. "Whether you're a fan of the music or not, your kids probably are," he said in a CNN interview about the new book in 2002.

LL's diligence as an actor in Hollywood finally paid off in 2003 with the release of the romantic comedy *Deliver Us From Eva*, his first major film in a starring role. In the movie, which was a retelling of the William Shakespeare play *Taming of the Shrew*, LL played opposite Gabrielle Union. LL's contribution to the movie attracted critical praise. *Premiere* magazine said that "overall, he delivers an immensely pleasing, touching performance."

LL appeared in four more movies over the next four years. The biggest of these were *S.W.A.T.*, the 2003 blockbuster in which he plays a member of an elite police unit, and the 2006 comedy *Last Holiday*, which also starred Queen Latifah. *Last Holiday* garnered positive views, including one from *Variety* magazine that praised LL's contribution. Building on his success, LL also set up his own movie production company, LL Cool J Inc., which landed a deal with Lions Gate Films in 2005. The film magazine *Daily Variety* reported that the terms of the multiyear contract were for several films, the first of which was slated to be a steamy thriller similar to the 2002 movie *Swimfan*.

LL Cool J is pictured in a New York bookstore promoting the children's book he wrote to help teach good sportsmanship. The Rawsistaz Reviewers said, "This is an excellent book that [we] would highly recommend for children."

In 2003 LL Cool J starred as an officer in an elite police S.W.A.T. team opposite Samuel L. Jackson and Colin Farrell. It was the second film the rapper starred in that year, although neither movie received particularly good reviews.

As if writing and acting were not adding enough to his plate, LL debuted his own clothing line, Todd Smith, in February 2006. He is no stranger to the world of fashion, having worked for several years as an endorser of the streetwear company FUBU. The Todd Smith line was a departure from typical fashion companies managed by hip-hop figures because it featured more formal clothes like overcoats and dinner jackets. LL made sure these garments were still reasonably priced. "I would like a person to look rich, to look successful but not be overly ornate," LL told MSNBC.com after the official release of the clothing line.

Still At It

What motivates someone who has accomplished so much? The answer for LL is simply to continue enjoying the work, whatever form it takes. "I love doing it all because I get to express myself artistically. It soothes and heals my soul," he told *Jet* magazine in 2002.

His passion was evident on the two albums he recorded after re-signing with Def Jam in 2003—*The DEFinition* and *Todd Smith*. After 10 studio albums, these recordings reflected a desire to continually evolve and stay original. "The challenge always becomes trying to do the best work you can, . . . trying to do something that's really exciting—and at the same time not repeating yourself," he told *Billboard* magazine in February 2006. The new LL had a dance-friendly bounce that fans had not heard from him before. This was partly the influence of the much sought-after rap producer Timbaland, who was involved with making both albums.

With the strong singles "Headsprung" and "Hush," *The DEFinition* hit record stores in August 2004, climbing to the number four spot on the *Billboard* album chart. "Headsprung" had a slow menacing vibe, and "Hush," a trademark "thug-love" rap, impressed *Billboard* magazine. *Rolling Stone* also praised the album, remarking that "the Cool J candy is as tasty as ever."

He hit the road after the release of *The DEFinition*, and his October performance at Radio City Music Hall won applause from the *New York Times*. The reviewer had fun observing how LL caters his show to his female fans—he is still eager to flex his huge muscles. "[A]t an LL Cool J show, men are little more than chaperones, and if any women objected to his throwing-out-roses routine, they didn't show it," reporter Kalefa Sanneh wrote.

Taking a very short break, LL came out with another album, *Todd Smith*, less than two years after the release of *The DEFinition*. Although its title implied a return to LL's old days as the lone rapper, the credits on *Todd Smith* reveal his openness to work with a wide range of guests, including singers Mary J. Blige, Ginuwine, and Jennifer Lopez, along

LL Cool J performs in New York City in March 2006. He remains one of the few early rappers still producing new music, and with his recent re-signing to Def Jam, LL will probably remain a force in the hip-hop world for many years.

with an all-star producer collective featuring Timbaland, Trackmasters, and the Neptunes' Pharrel Williams. The decision to pair up with Jennifer Lopez on the first single, the techno-inspired "Control Myself," was a no-brainer, considering their success with the "All I Have" duet a few years earlier. "Control Myself" made *Billboard*'s Hot 100 chart, and the music video for the song climbed all the way to the number two spot on the MTV show *Total Request Live.*

Today, LL Cool J's reign at the top of the hip-hop world is undisputable. Even the rappers who first inspired him to pick up the mic have given him due credit. Grandmaster Flash, who with the Furious Five recorded "Freedom" when LL was only 12, has stated his respect for LL's style: "Love songs? Ain't too many cats who could touch 'em with that." Rick Rubin has called LL's rhymes groundbreaking: "He's the first MC to really take the lyric writing to another level." Darryl McDaniels, better known as DMC of Run-D.M.C., summed it up nicely: "No one can take his crown."

Album after album, year after year, LL Cool J has continued to prove himself. Once a skinny 16-year-old without a label, he went on to become one of hip-hop's originators. He made his share of mistakes while racking up the hits, but he learned from many from them. Now an outspoken veteran, he's one of hip-hop's main defenders, harnessing its power for good. More than two decades in the game, James Todd Smith is still conquering, rhyming, and inspiring. And he's just gettin' warm.

1968 James Todd Smith is born on January 14 in Long Island, New York.

1979 He attends his first Sugarhill Gang concert at the Harlem Armory.

1982 Ladies Love Cool J starts performing at block parties with friend Jay Philpot.

1984 He sends a demo to hip-hop producer Rick Rubin, who teams up with Russell Simmons to release "I Need a Beat," Def Jam's first record.

1985 LL releases his first album, *Radio*, and makes a cameo appearance in the film *Krush Groove*.

1986 *Radio* goes gold, and LL appears in the movie *Wildcats*.

1987 He meets Simone, his future wife, and releases *Bigger and Deffer*.

1988 LL records "Going Back to Cali" for the *Less Than Zero* soundtrack.

1989 LL Cool J releases *Walking With a Panther*. Simone gives birth to a son named Najee.

1990 LL finds mainstream success with his fourth album, *Mama Said Knock You Out*, which features chart-topping songs "Mama Said Knock You Out" and "Around the Way Girl." His daughter, Italia, is born.

1991 He performs on the MTV show *Unplugged* and lands small role in the movie *The Hard Way*.

1992 The rapper wins his first Grammy for Best Rap Solo performance and opens up Camp Cool J for disadvantaged inner-city kids.

1993 LL takes part in formation of AmeriCorps, a national volunteer organization. He also releases *14 Shots to the Dome*.

1995 The album *Mr. Smith* is released. LL stars in a new TV sitcom *In the House*. He marries Simone, and his daughter Samaria is born.

1997 LL receives his second Grammy and releases his greatest hits album, *All World*. The album *Phenomenon* is released, and LL publishes his autobiography, *I Make My Own Rules*.

1998 He appears in the urban thriller *Caught Up*, the romantic comedy *Woo*, and the horror flick *Halloween H20*.

1999 The last episode of *In the House* airs. LL lands roles in three more movies, including the blockbuster *Any Given Sunday*.

2000 *G.O.A.T. Featuring James T. Smith: The Greatest of All Time* is released. LL's daughter Nina Simone Beautiful is born.

2001 LL Cool J attends the first Hip-Hop Summit in New York City.

2002 The album *10* is released, and LL's children's book, *And the Winner Is*, is published.

2003 LL costars in *Deliver Us From Eva* and *S.W.A.T.* He also re-signs with Def Jam.

2004 *The DEFinition* is released.

2005 LL performs and is paid tribute at the VH1 *2nd Annual Hip-Hop Honors*.

2006 He costars in *Last Holiday* starring Queen Latifah and unveils Todd Smith clothing line. He also releases *Todd Smith*.

2007 LL releases *Exit 13*.

Top Ten Singles
1987 "I'm Bad"
     "I Need Love"
1989 "I'm That Type of Guy"
1990 "The Boomin' System"
     "Jingling Baby"
1991 "Mama Said Knock You Out"
     "Around the Way Girl"
     "6 Minutes of Pleasure"
1993 "Back Seat (Of My Jeep)"
1995 "Hey Lover"
1996 "Loungin"
     "Doin It"
1997 "Ain't Nobody"
     "4, 3, 2, 1"
1998 "Father"
2002 "Luv U Better"
     "All I Have" (Jennifer Lopez featuring LL Cool J)
2003 "Paradise"
2004 "Headsprung"

Albums
1985 *Radio*
1987 *Bigger and Deffer*
1990 *Mama Said Knock You Out*
1993 *14 Shots to the Dome*
1995 *Mr. Smith*
1996 *All World: Greatest Hits*
1997 *Phenomenon*
2000 *G.O.A.T. Featuring James T. Smith: The Greatest of All Time*
2002 *10*
2004 *The DEFinition*
2006 *Todd Smith*
2007 *Exit 13*

Films
1985 *Krush Groove*
1986 *Wildcats*
1991 *The Hard Way*

1992 *Toys*
1995 *Out-of-Sync*
1996 *The Right to Remain Silent*
1998 *Caught Up*
Woo
Halloween H20: 20 Years Later
1999 *Deep Blue Sea*
In Too Deep
Any Given Sunday
2000 *Charlie's Angels*
2001 *Kingdom Come*
2002 *Rollerball*
2003 *Deliver Us from Eva*
S.W.A.T.
2004 *Mindhunters*
2005 *Edison*
Slow Burn
2006 *Last Holiday*
2007 *Slow Burn*

Television
1995–
1999 *In the House*
2005 VH1 *2nd Annual Hip-Hop Honors Show*

Awards
1992 Grammy for Best Rap Solo Performance for "Mama Said Knock You Out"
1996 NAACP Image Award—Best Rap Artist
1997 Grammy for Best Rap Solo Performance for "Hey Lover"
MTV Video Music Vanguard Award for career achievement
2001 NAACP Image Award—Outstanding Rap Artist
2003 Soul Train Quincy Jones Award
NAACP Image Award—Outstanding Male Artist
Source Foundation Image Award

Service Organizations
AmeriCorps
Camp Cool J

Books

Chappell, Kevin. "LL Cool J Turns Up the Heat and Talks About Love, Marriage and Why He Gave Up 'The Naked Look.'" *Ebony* 58, no. 3: 116–20.

Gueraseva, Stacy. *Def Jam, Inc.* New York: Random House, 2005.

LL Cool J. *And The Winner Is . . .* New York: Scholastic, 2002.

———. *I Make My Own Rules.* New York: St. Martin's Press, 1997.

Light, Alan, ed. *The Vibe History of Hip Hop.* New York: Three Rivers Press, 1999.

Ogg, Alex. *The Men Behind Def Jam.* London: Omnibus Press, 2002.

Osario, Kim. "Built to Last." *The Source* no. 159: 148–156.

Pareles, Jon. "LL Cool J Tries to Find A Way Back." *New York Times* (October 14, 2002): E5.

Sanneh, Kelefa. "Two Hip-Hop Pioneers, Still True to Form." *New York Times* (October 11, 2004): E1, E6.

Web Sites

LL Cool J Official Web Site Page
www.defjam.com
The Def Jam Web site includes an official profile of LL Cool J as well as notices of upcoming album releases and public appearances.

MTV LL Cool J Timeline
http://www.mtv.com/bands/archive/l/ll_cool_j/llcoolj_index.jhtml
A timeline of LL Cool J that highlights his albums and musical achievements.

VH1 Hip-Hop Honors Page
http://www.vh1.com/shows/events/hip_hop_honors/2005
This VH1 page covers the *Hip-Hop Honors 2005* show, which recognized LL Cool J and other legends. Under the "Honorees" heading, you can find an interactive page of LL Cool J or another artist as well as video clips from the show.

Hip-Hop Action Network
www.hsan.org
The official Web site of the Hip-Hop Action Network, which has become a political action committee since its first summit in 2001.

AmeriCorps Homepage
www.americorps.org
This Web site for AmeriCorps explains its mission and includes opportunities to get involved in its programs.

civil—behaving in a courteous or polite manner.

exhortation—the act of giving warning or advice.

explicit—open in the depiction of sexual content.

G.E.D.—an acronym for General Education Development, a test for individuals who did not complete their high school diploma. G.E.D. can also stand for General Equivalency Diploma, which is an alternate to a high school degree awarded to those who pass the G.E.D. test.

genre—a category of art, music, or literature characterized by a particular style.

holistic—concerned with the complete system. A holistic approach to solving a problem does not break down a person, situation, or system into parts to try to determine a singular cause.

humanitarian—a person working toward the welfare of people.

introspection—the internal process of examining one's own thoughts and feelings.

memoir—an autobiography.

mescaline—a hallucinatory drug.

novice—a beginner.

parlay—to increase or otherwise transform into something of much greater value.

tenant—one who rents or leases from a landlord.

versatile—turning with ease from one thing to another.

abuse, 13, 16–17, 40–41
acting career, 26, 29, 32–33, 41, 43, 50, 52
"All I Have," 45, 55
And the Winner Is, 50–51
Any Given Sunday, 43

"Big Mama (Unconditional Love)", 45, 47
Bigger and Deffer, 12–13, 20, 22
Blige, Mary J., 53
Boyz II Men, 32
Brown, Foxy, 32

Camp Cool J, 26
"Candy," 37
Canibus, 38
Caught Up, 41
Cohen, Lyor, 32
Combs, Sean "Diddy," 10, 47
"Control Myself," 55
Cut Creator, 10, 20

Deep Blue Sea, 43
Def Jam, 10, 12, 18–21, 32, 48, 49–50, 53
The DEFinition, 53
Deliver Us from Eva, 33, 50
DJ Scratch, 44
DMX, 12, 38, 44
"Doin It," 32
Dorsey, Marc, 45

Fat Joe, 32
"Father," 37–39
Fisher, Charles, 26, 28, 32
14 Shots to the Dome, 28–29

gangsta rap, 25
Ginuwine, 53
G.O.A.T. Featuring James T. Smith: The Greatest of All Time, 44–45

"Going Back to Cali," 23
Grammy awards, 12, 26, 27, 33, 35, 49
Grandmaster Flash & the Furious Five, 9–10, 55
Griffin, Ellen and Eugene, 15–16, 19–20, 25, 47

Halloween H20, 41
The Hard Way, 26
"Headsprung," 53
"Hey Lover," 32–33
Hip-Hop Honors (VH1), 8–11
Hip-Hop Summit, 47
Hunter, Karen, 40
   See also *I Make My Own Rules* (LL Cool J and Karen Hunter)
"Hush," 53

"I Can't Live Without My Radio," 18
I Make My Own Rules (LL Cool J and Karen Hunter), 16–17, 36–37, 38, 40–41
"I Need a Beat," 18
"I Need Love," 13, 20–21, 45
"I Shot Ya," 32
Ice-T, 9, 10, 25, 38
In the House, 32, 41
In Too Deep, 43

Ja Rule, 44
Johnson, Simone (spouse), 21, 23, 30–31
   See also marriage and family life
Jones, Quincy, 32

Kool Moe Dee, 38

Ladies Love Cool James. *See* LL Cool J
Last Holiday, 50
Lighty, Chris, 32

LL Cool J
  and abuse, 13, 16–17, 40–41
  acting career (film), 26, 29, 33, 41, 43, 50, 52
  acting career (television), 32, 41
  awards won by, 12, 20, 26, 27, 33, 35, 49
  charity work, 26, 28, 35
  childhood of, 14–17
  clothing line, 52–53
  with Def Jam, 10, 12–13, 18–21, 25–27, 32, 48–50, 53–55
  drops out of school, 20, 29
  and drugs, 23
  early music, 18–20
  enrolls in G.E.D. program, 31
  influence of, 8–13, 55
  marriage and family life, 21, 23, 26, 28–29, 30–31, 39, 44
  and money management, 21–23, 29
  number of albums, 10, 12–13, 37, 44–45
  positive message of, 44–47
LL Cool J Inc., 50
Lopez, Jennifer, 45, 53, 55
"Loungin," 32
"Luv U Better," 45, 49

Mama Said Knock You Out, 9, 12–13, 24–26, 27
Marley Marl, 26
marriage and family life, 21, 23, 26, 28–29, 30–31, 39, 44
McDaniels, Darryl, 55
Method Man, 38, 44
Mr. Smith, 13, 32–35, 37

NAACP Image Awards, 49
Nelly, 10, 11
Neptunes, 44–45, 55
N.W.A, 25

Out-of-Sync, 29, 41

Phenomenon, 36–38
Philpot, Jay, 16, 18

Queen Latifah, 10, 50

R. Kelly, 35
Radio, 12, 18–19
Redman, 38, 44
"The Ripper Strikes Back," 38
Rubin, Rick, 10, 18–19, 20–21, 55
Run-D.M.C., 18, 25, 55

Sanneh, Kalefa, 53
Shakur, Tupac, 41
Simmons, Russell, 10, 12, 18–19, 20–21, 26, 47, 48–49
Smith, James (father), 15–16, 23
Smith, James Todd. *See* LL Cool J
Smith, Ondrea (mother), 14–16, 22–23
Smith, Will, 32, 33
Snoop Dogg, 44
Soul Train Music Awards, 20, 49
The Source, 22, 38, 42, 44
S.W.A.T., 50, 52

10, 13, 44–45, 47
Timbaland, 53, 55
Todd Smith, 12, 53, 55
Todd Smith (clothing line), 52–53
Total Request Live (MTV), 55
Toys, 26
Trackmasters, 32, 55

Unplugged (MTV), 26

Walking With a Panther, 23, 25
Williams, Pharrel, 55
Woo, 41

Youth Enterprises, 26

Brian Baughan is a writer and editor who lives in Philadelphia. He is the author of *Human Rights in Africa* and *Liberia*, and served as contributing editor to two study guides in Howard Bloom's MAJOR SHORT STORY WRITERS series. During the writing of this book, Brian's stereo had "Rock the Bells" on repeat.

Picture Credits

page

2: Zuma Press/Steven Tackeff	**33:** Mario Anzuoni/Splash News
8: Reuters/Seth Wenig	**34:** Zuma Press/Def Jam
11: Reuters/Seth Wenig	**36:** Zuma Press/Steven Tackeff
12: Mel Nudelman/ PRNewsFoto/NMI	**39:** UPI/Michael Germana
14: Zuma Press/Def Jam	**40:** UPI/Ezio Petersen
17: NMI/Michelle Feng	**42:** NMI/Michelle Feng
19: Zuma Press/Rahav Segev	**43:** Warner Bros./Zuma Press
20: AP Photo/Bob Galbraith	**45:** Zuma Press/Steven Tackeff
21: KRT/Olivier Douliery	**46:** UPI/Ezio Petersen
22: Zuma Press/Toronto Star	**48:** UPI/Ezio Petersen
24: Zuma Press/Def Jam	**51:** Alecsey Boldeskul/ NY Photo Press
27: Sam Mircovich]/Reuters	**52:** Columbia Pictures/Zuma Press
28: Zuma Press/Def Jam	**54:** Janet Mayer/Splash News
30: Tom Lau/Loud & Clear/Star Max	

Front cover: UPI/Robin Platzer
Back cover: KRT/Lionel Hahn